THE YEAR OF YOU

365 JOURNAL WRITING PROMPTS FOR CREATIVE SELF-DISCOVERY

HANNAH BRAIME

INDIVIDUATE PRESS

The Year of You: 365 Journal Writing Prompts for Creative Self-Discovery

© 2017 Hannah Braime

ISBN: 978-1916059146

Published by Individuate Press

Cover design: Danijela Mijailovic

Image credit: Freepik

CONTENTS

WELCOME

Welcome to The Year of You! I want to take you on a journey of self-discovery over the next 365 days using a single journaling prompt each day. Over the course of 12 months, we'll unpack the important areas of your life, from relationships and identity to money, career, and health. The prompts I will share with you in this book are short and simple, but thought-provoking and sometimes even fun! You'll have the chance to explore your life on all kinds of levels, from your deepest hopes, dreams, fears, and secrets, to personal trivia and future adventures.

I created this book because I know how powerful a regular journaling habit is. As well as the obvious benefits, like increasing self-awareness and creativity, research has also suggested regular journaling improves your memory, physical health and problem-solving abilities, as well as reducing stress. I also know from experience how useful it can be to have some kind of structure to follow as you cultivate or strengthen a new habit. Using this book, all you need to do is turn to today's date, read the prompt, and write. Before you know it, you'll be writing regularly, if not daily, and making time for valuable self-connection, reflection, and growth.

How to use this book

There are two ways you can use this book, depending on where in the year you are as you read this.

1. **Start on 1st January.** If the new year is upon you or right around the corner, perfect! You can begin with the first day of chapter one and continue from there.
2. **Start wherever you are today.** As you'll see, each chapter in this book corresponds with a month of the year; chapter one is January, chapter two February, and so on. Each chapter also has the same number of prompts as there are days in that month. But this doesn't mean you need to work through the chapters from the beginning. If you're starting this on February 5th, you can turn straight to chapter two and begin on the prompt for today's date. If you're beginning on November 29th, ditto.

Chapter 13, "Looking back on a year of you" is for reading after you've completed a full year of journaling and all the prompts in the book (or as many as you choose). If you start 'in media res,' save this chapter until you have completed all 12 months.

I've endeavored to make the prompts in this book clear and concise and have deliberately avoided adding my own remarks and notes to each question (except in a couple of instances where I've mentioned specific resources or suggestions). I appreciate, however, you will be reading this book with different frames of reference, experience, and perspective from me. So, if you encounter any prompts whose meaning seems ambiguous, I encourage you to go with what you *think* it means (or what you'd like it to mean).

At the end of each month, you'll see an opportunity to review and reflect on your journaling entries for that month. Reading back over past journaling is a valuable exercise. It's not always the most comfortable one though! If you feel resistance to reflecting on previous journal entries, I invite you to be gentle with yourself and get curious about where that resistance is coming from. What are the thoughts and feelings behind it?

One principle I like to share with fellow journalers and coaching clients is *journaling is whatever you want it to be*. While certain practices and habits will make your journaling more or less helpful and enjoyable, there are no rules and no "right" way to journal. That means if you want to mix up the prompts in this book and choose the one that resonates most with you on any day, go for it. Reflecting at the end of each month is helpful, but if you'd rather skip this, that's fine too. The only caveat I'd add is it's important to notice when we might avoid a particular topic or question and ask ourselves what we're avoiding and why.

Creating the journaling habit

A 365-day habit might sound daunting, but it is possible with a few tips and tricks and by taking one day at a time:

- **Try to journal at the same time each day.** Ideally, the morning since if you're unable to do your writing then, you still have the rest of the day to catch up.
- **Don't stress if you miss a day (or five).** The prompts will still be there for you when you're ready to get back to writing. We all fall off the wagon, break a streak, etc. What matters most isn't falling off the wagon, it's how quickly you can get back on again afterward. The discomfort of staying off is often much greater and more draining than biting the bullet and re-starting. At the same time...

- **Any journaling is better than no journaling.** If you don't have time to write for 20 minutes, write for two.
- **Start with the "just 5 minutes" rule.** Set a goal for yourself to journal for just five minutes every day. Give yourself permission to stop journaling after those five minutes. You can carry on if you're having a good time, but keeping your journaling fun and pleasant (rather than a "should" or an obligation) will make you more likely to stick to the habit.

What you need to get started

One of the great things about journaling is you probably already have everything you need to begin. Here are the main ingredients that are helpful:

- A pen and notebook or computer/tablet/phone.
- A space to journal: make it somewhere pleasant and comfortable; somewhere you want to go to journal each day. Doing it in the same place will help you get in the right headspace.
- An open mind. Practice shelving your judgments of yourself as you write.

You can learn more about the basics of journaling and creating a practice that works for you in my book *The Ultimate Guide to Journaling*. I've also included a list of my favorite journaling apps and software in the section called "Additional Resources and Recommended Reading" at the end of this book.

For now, the most important thing you can do is *start*. With that in mind, let's dive in straight away with your first prompts...

PART 1
JANUARY: IDENTITY

January 1st

What are the different roles you play in your life (e.g. mother, partner, sister, etc.) List as many as you can think of.

January 2nd

What roles do you hope to play in the future?

January 3rd

What are some of your most important rules for living?

January 4th

What are your top five core values?

Core values are the qualities and experiences that are most important to us to embody and have present in our lives. These might include things like trust, love, connection, freedom, growth, etc. If you're not already with your core values, you will find comprehensive lists of values with a quick Google search. I also share a free workbook called "Discover Your Values," which guides you through this process in the Becoming Who You Are Library, which you can find at: http://bit.ly/bwyacommunity.

January 5th

What are your core strengths?

If you're not familiar with the concept of personal strengths (or it's been a while since you measured yours), you can take the free VIA strengths test to find out. Find this by googling "VIA strengths test" or use the URL in the resources section of this book.

January 6th

How are you most often misunderstood? Why do you think
this is?

January 7th

What are you most proud of about your life right now?

January 8th

What do you consider to be your biggest challenge in life?

January 9th

Out of the different areas of life covered in each month of this book, which are well attended, and which could use a little more TLC over the coming months?

January 10th

What makes you who you are?

January 11th

What do you wish more people knew about you?

January 12th

What annoys you about other people? How does that trait or behavior show up in your personality and your life?

January 13th

What does happiness mean to you?

January 14th

How connected to yourself and your body do you feel today?

January 15th

What scares you?

January 16th

How is your life different today to how you imagined it would be when you were younger?

January 17th

What are the most important qualities you aspire to embody in your day-to-day life?

January 18th

How do you think other people would describe you if asked?

January 19th

What is one thing you secretly hope other people don't discover or find out about you?

January 20th

Would you describe your glass as half full or half empty?

January 21st

How do you feel about your age?

January 22nd

What is one thing you would like to change about your present self?

January 23rd

What is one quality you embody today you hope you keep for the rest of your life?

January 24th

What is your biggest goal right now?

January 25th

Where are you today? Is this where you want to be, or is there someplace else you'd rather be?

January 26th

What is the number one thing you are grateful for today?

January 27th

What is your present self most excited about?

January 28th

What do you know to be true about yourself?

January 29th

What is an unpopular opinion or belief you have?

January 30th

What recharges your batteries more: alone time or socializing with other people?

January 31st

What is it like being you today?

LOOKING BACK ON JANUARY

We've started the year by exploring the different ingredients that make you *you*, the things that make you tick, and fun personal trivia. As you reach the end of this month, this is a good opportunity to look back at your answers to January's questions and ask:

- What did I learn about myself this month?
- Which of this month's prompts were most challenging?
- Which of my answers most surprised me?
- Based on what I've written, one action I want to take over the next month is…

PART 2
FEBRUARY: THE PAST

February 1st

Name five key events that have shaped your life and who you
are today.

February 2nd

Name five people who have had a profound impact on your life.

February 3rd

Think of a big decision you made in your past and imagine you made an alternative choice. What would your life be like now?

February 4th

Describe your earliest memory.

February 5th

If you had to give the five-minute summary of your life so far to someone who didn't know you, what would you tell them?

February 6th

What from your past do you feel most proud of?

February 7th

What do you struggle to accept from your past?

February 8th

What from your past feels unresolved?

February 9th

Choose a photo from your past. Write the thoughts and
feelings that come to mind as you look at it.

February 10th

How do you view the past versions of yourself from each decade of your life so far?

February 11th

What incident from your past would you least like people in your life today to know about?

February 12th

How do you think the you of today is different to the you from 10 years ago?

February 13th

Write the first memory that comes to mind associated with each of these words (or, if time is tight, choose one):

- magic
- freedom
- conversation
- joy

February 14th

What do you remember (or imagine) being worried about 10 years ago?

February 15th

What is a belief you were raised with that you now disagree with?

February 16th

What is a rule or principle you disagreed with or rebelled against growing up you now agree with or know to be true?

February 17th

How has your past made you a better person in the present?

February 18th

When you think of "the past," what images or memories come to mind?

February 19th

What advice do you have for yourself from 10 years ago?

February 20th

Make a list of the places from your past would you most like
to return to.

February 21st

Which people from your past would you most love to see again?

February 22nd

When in the past have you been true to yourself and your values, even in the face of opposition or difficulty?

February 23rd

When in the past have you not been true to yourself?

February 24th

What is one of the biggest mistakes your past self has made, and what did you learn from it?

February 25th

How do you think your past defines who you are today?

February 26th

If you could go back and relive the last year, what would you do differently?

February 27th

Think back to an important world event. Where were you
when it happened, what were you doing?

February 28th

Write the first memory that comes to mind associated with each of these words (or if time is tight, choose one):

- birthday
- hug
- school
- family

February 29th

What is a missed opportunity from your past you wish you'd taken?

FEBRUARY IN REVIEW

Having explored your identity during January, this month we've taken a detour into the past. While our pasts don't define us, there is no doubt they influence who we are in the present: our emotional experiences, the choices we make, how we respond to situations, and more. As we approach the end of this month, hopefully, you have a better idea of how your past has influenced you, the key milestones of your life so far, and you have taken a few nostalgic trips down memory lane...

Here are a few questions to consider as you review your journaling from this month:

- What did I learn about myself this month?
- Which of this month's prompts were most challenging?
- Which of my answers most surprised me?
- Based on what I've written, one action I want to take over the next month is...

PART 3
MARCH: ENVIRONMENT

March 1st

Where do you live?

March 2nd

What's the view like from where you are right now?

March 3rd

What in your environment today could you not imagine living
without?

March 4th

What wouldn't you miss if it were gone tomorrow?

March 5th

What material possessions have sentimental value to you? Why?

March 6th

Do you own your home? Why, or why not?

March 7th

How do you take care of your environment?

March 8th

Where would you prefer to live: mountains or beach? Why?

March 9th

If you lost everything you have tomorrow, what would you add back into your home first?

March 10th

How do you feel about your current environment?

March 11th

What are your top considerations when purchasing everyday items (e.g. price, aesthetic, quality, vibe, something else)?

March 12th

What colors do you surround yourself with on a daily basis?

March 13th

What is more important to you: style or comfort? Why?

March 14th

For your environment, do you subscribe to the idea "less is more," or do you like to surround yourself with belongings?

March 15th

If you could tear it all down and start again, what would you create differently in your current environment?

March 16th

What is the number one thing missing from your environment right now?

March 17th

Which season is your favorite and why?

March 18th

What words would you use to describe your ideal home?

March 19th

What does "home" mean to you? Spend 10 minutes free writing on this topic.

March 20th

Do you prefer to live alone or with others? Why (and if it's the latter who)?

March 21st

What is one thing you can change in your environment today
to make it more pleasing to you?

March 22nd

Are you a city or country person? Why?

March 23rd

What are you most grateful for about your home right now?

March 24th

How does your environment influence your mood? What can you learn from that?

March 25th

In which environments or places do you feel most at home?

March 26th

What stories do you think the walls in your current home
would tell?

March 27th

If you were to make your current environment 5% more comfortable, what would you do?

March 28th

Make a list of 10 things you like about your current environment and 10 things you'd like to change.

March 29th

What do you worry about most when it comes to your environment?

March 30th

What are your favorite noises? And your least favorite?

March 31st

What energizes you more: spending time alone or spending time with other people?

REFLECTING ON MARCH

Our environment can have a huge impact on our day-to-day experience of life, and that's what we've been focusing on this month. You've had the chance to consider all aspects of your physical environment, from your home to your broader environment, the climate and weather, and more. As you review your journaling from this month, here are a few questions to consider:

- What did I learn about myself this month?
- Which of the prompts this month were most challenging?
- Which of my answers most surprised me?
- Based on what I've written, one action I want to take over the next month is…

PART 4
APRIL: FUN

April 1st

What does fun mean to you?

April 2nd

Is fun something that comes easily to you?

April 3rd

What would your ideal day look like?

April 4th

Make a list of 20 things that make you smile and/or laugh.

April 5th

What is your go-to entertainment of choice?

April 6th

What is the best movie you've ever seen? Why?

April 7th

If you had the opportunity to be one of the first people to colonize the moon or another planet, would you take it?

April 8th

What is your favorite way to relax?

April 9th

What is one of your most fun memories from childhood?

April 10th

What are your favorite books and why?

April 11th

What excites you about life right now?

April 12th

How can you add more spontaneity and excitement to your life today?

April 13th

Imagine you had to show a young child what fun was all about. What would you say and do to show them?

April 14th

Make a list of 10 fun things to do on a rainy day.

April 15th

What are some of the most common excuses or reasons you give about why you can't do the things you want to do?

April 16th

What new hobbies would you love to try?

April 17th

Which TV shows have you seen every episode of?

April 18th

What fun activity do you have the urge to do today?

April 19th

What are your biggest time-wasters or energy drains right now?

April 20th

Who are your favorite people to hang out with?

April 21st

What is the best concert you've ever been to?

April 22nd

What brings you joy?

April 23rd

When was the last time you were silly? What happened? How did it feel?

April 24th

Make a list of 10 possible things you could do next time you feel bored.

April 25th

What would your dream day off look like?

April 26th

What is your favorite kind of music and why?

April 27th

Are you an outdoors or indoors person? What is your favorite activity in either setting?

April 28th

What would your perfect Sunday afternoon look like?

April 29th

If your life were turned into a movie, what would it be called and what genre would it be?

April 30th

What is one fun thing you'd like to experience during your lifetime you haven't yet?

April 31st

How can you add 5% more fun to your life today?

LOOKING BACK ON APRIL

In a culture where busy-ness is a virtue and over-commitment is the norm, this month is intended to bring you back to an important but often-overlooked aspect of your existence: fun! You've explored your relationship to fun, how you most enjoy spending your time and brainstormed ways to add more fun to your daily life. As you reflect on your journaling entries for this month, here are a few questions to consider:

- What did I learn about myself this month?
- Which of the prompts this month were most challenging?
- Which of my answers most surprised me?
- Based on what I've written, one action I want to take over the next month is...

PART 5
MAY: CAREER

May 1st

How do you answer the question "What do you do?"

May 2nd

What have the highlights of your career path been up to this point?

May 3rd

If you were free to do whatever you wanted to do as a career, with no judgment or repercussions, what would you do?

May 4th

What does success mean to you? Do you consider yourself to
be successful?

May 5th

How much money do you earn? How much would you like to earn?

May 6th

What do you consider to be your biggest career achievement so far?

May 7th

Would you prefer to be a jack-of-all-trades or a master of one?

May 8th

What do you need to believe about yourself and about the world to make your biggest goals and dreams a reality?

May 9th

What do you love to do so much you would pay (or do pay) to do it?

May 10th

Think of a big goal you're working towards at the moment (or aspiring towards). How will you know when you've reached or completed it?

May 11th

What, to you, is the difference between work and play?

May 12th

What opportunities do you currently have within your career?
What opportunities would you like to have?

May 13th

What motivates you? What helps you stay on track with your
goals and ambitions?

May 14th

How important is your career to you, and why?

May 15th

What are you passionate about?

May 16th

If you could go back to day one and begin again, what would you do differently in your career?

May 17th

What would you like your contribution to the world to be?

May 18th

Where in your career could you use support right now?

May 19th

Describe one of your career goals. What is one thing you can do today to bring yourself closer to that goal?

May 20th

What is your biggest source of career stress today?

May 21st

Where are you procrastinating right now?

May 22nd

Do you believe work/life balance exists?

May 23rd

Are you more of a team player or a lone wolf?

May 24th

What is the most valuable lesson you've learned in your career so far?

May 25th

What would you do differently if you were to bring a deeper level of authenticity to your work?

May 26th

If you could choose one area in which to deepen your expertise, what would it be?

May 27th

What did you want to be when you were younger?

May 28th

What careers do you imagine for yourself "when you grow up" now?

May 29th

What are you fantastic at? What are some of your strongest skills and talents?

May 30th

What did your parents do for a career? How have their choices influenced your own?

May 31st

What would an ideal workday look like to you?

MAY: A REVIEW

This month, we've explored an area that, for many of us, is what gives our lives a sense of purpose and meaning... or doesn't. Our careers can be a source of joy, wealth, pain, uncertainty, stress, and so much more. No doubt you had several ideas about what you wanted to do and who you wanted to be when you grew up (maybe, like me, you still do!), but how does that compare to reality? Is your career something that, overall, adds to your life, or is it a drain? Where are your opportunities for growth? Where can you build on your strengths? These are all questions you've approached in one way or another over the last 31 days. As you review your responses this month, here are a few questions to consider:

- What did I learn about myself this month?
- Which of the prompts this month were most challenging?
- Which of my answers most surprised me?
- Based on what I've written, one action I want to take over the next month is...

PART 6

JUNE: RELATIONSHIPS

June 1st

How satisfied are you with your social life?

June 2nd

How easy or hard do you find asking for help when you
need it?

June 3rd

What does family mean to you?

June 4th

What do you think of when you think about love?

June 5th

Do you tend to hold a grudge or to forgive and forget?

June 6th

What do you enjoy doing for other people?

June 7th

How do you feel about your current relationship status?

June 8th

How do you feel about having children?

June 9th

When was the last time you went on a date?

June 10th

What qualities do you believe are most important in
friendships?

June 11th

Who do you consider to be your closest friend? How did you meet? What do you appreciate about your friendship?

June 12th

Describe a recent compliment or piece of positive feedback you received that was meaningful to you.

June 13th

What was the last compliment or piece of positive feedback you remember giving?

June 14th

How do you feel about gossip?

June 15th

How would you like to be seen by those closest to you?

June 16th

Do you believe you are lucky or unlucky in love? What informs that belief?

June 17th

What did you imagine your relationships would be like at this stage of your life when you were younger?

June 18th

Describe a time when you helped a friend in need.

June 19th

How compassionate do you think you are towards other people in your life? Do you extend that compassion to yourself?

June 20th

What, for you, is the difference between "like" and "love?"

June 21st

What assumptions do you make about other people most often?

June 22nd

What does your happy ever after look like?

June 23rd

What does good communication in a relationship look like to you?

June 24th

How do you deal with conflict?

June 25th

What were you raised to believe about sex? Have these
beliefs changed? If so, how?

June 26th

Make a list of your favorite people.

To take this question one step further, create a visual. Draw a circle and write your name in the center. Draw another bigger circle around the outside of that and write the names of your closest friends inside. Then, draw a third circle around the first two. Write the names of your close-but-not-closest friends, and so on. You can create as many circles as you want based on your own criteria. Once you're finished, take a look and notice: which circles are rich with people? And which circles could use a few more friendly faces?

June 27th

Think of your closest relationship right now. What is one thing you could do today to make that relationship more satisfying and harmonious?

June 28th

What feels unforgivable to you in a relationship?

June 29th

How do you express feelings like anger and hurt?

June 30th

What relationships would you like to develop further over the next six months? Who else would you like to meet?

REFLECTING ON JUNE

Quality relationships are pivotal to our wellbeing. Several studies have shown a connection between having strong relationships and living longer. A good level of social connection has also been linked with improved physical and mental health: better immune function, better cardiovascular health, deeper resilience, and heightened positivity.

This month, we've explored what good relationships look like to you, what qualities are crucial, and how you can bring a deeper level of satisfaction to your most important relationships. Here are a few additional questions to consider as you look back on your answers from this month:

- What did I learn about myself this month?
- Which of this month's prompts were most challenging?
- Which of my answers most surprised me?
- Based on what I've written, one action I want to take over the next month is...

PART 7
JULY: GROWTH

July 1st

What is the number one thing that, if you started doing it today, would have the biggest positive impact on your life?

July 2nd

What is the number one thing that, if you stopped doing it today, would have the biggest positive impact on your life?

July 3rd

What's the number one thing that feels like it's missing from your life right now?

July 4th

How do you measure personal growth? How do you know when you've grown as a person?

July 5th

In which areas of your life would you like to see growth over the next 12 months?

July 6th

Which books have had the biggest impact on your life?

July 7th

What is your favourite way to learn new things?

July 8th

What is the number one thing you would like to change about your life right now?

July 9th

What is the number one thing you struggle to accept about yourself but would like to do so?

July 10th

Do you typically run late, early, or on time, and what do you think this reflects about you?

July 11th

What emotions do you find it hardest to accept within yourself?

July 12th

In which area of your life have you experienced the most growth recently? Why?

July 13th

In which area of your life have you experienced the least growth recently? What would you like to do about this?

July 14th

What is one thing you could learn more about that would improve your life?

July 15th

What are you currently saying yes to that you'd like to say
no to?

July 16th

And what are you currently saying no to that you'd like to say yes to?

July 17th

What do you need to hear today? What do you want to tell yourself?

July 18th

What is the kindest thing you could do for yourself today?

July 19th

How have your past experiences have prepared you for the life you're living today?

July 20th

Describe a decision you're facing right now. Which path will lead to most growth?

July 21st

How do you balance self-acceptance and self-improvement?

July 22nd

Describe a recurring pattern in your life you'd like to change.

July 23rd

Describe an event, situation, or person from your past that became a catalyst for growth.

July 24th

If you knew you had one more year left to live, what would you change about your life today?

July 25th

What is one negative story you tell yourself about yourself
that holds you back?

July 26th

If you were 5% more true to yourself and your core values today, what would you do differently?

July 27th

What are you avoiding in your life right now? What would it look like to face it head on?

July 28th

Describe something you've done in your life you didn't think you could do. What did you learn from this?

July 29th

Write an unsent letter to someone with whom you want to make amends.

July 30th

What are three things you'd do if you weren't afraid to do them?

July 31st

What tools or practices (for example, journaling) do you use
to help your growth?

LOOKING BACK ON JULY

I'll take a guess that if you're working through this book you're interested in personal growth! The last 31 prompts were all about self-awareness, self-understanding, and self-responsibility: three key pillars of personal growth. As you might have experienced in previous chapters, taking a deep look at ourselves isn't always the most comfortable experience. With any of your journaling, go as far as you want, be gentle, and remember even asking yourself the question is a valuable act, however much and whatever you write in response.

Here are a few questions to think about as you review your answers this month:

What did I learn about myself this month?

- Which of the prompts this month were most challenging?
- Which of my answers most surprised me?
- Based on what I've written, one action I want to take over the next month is…

PART 8
AUGUST: MONEY

August 1st

Describe your relationship with money in five words or less.

August 2nd

What was your money story growing up?

August 3rd

What is your money story today?

August 4th

What does it mean to you to have "not enough" money?

August 5th

Is there such a thing as "too much" money? Do you think you
have a money ceiling?

August 6th

What, to you, is the purpose of money?

August 7th

How would you like to feel about money?

August 8th

What is your biggest fear in relation to money?

August 9th

How does money bring you joy?

August 10th

If you found $500 today, what would you do with it?

August 11th

Have you ever lost a lot of money or made a big purchase you later regretted?

August 12th

What would a 100% positive relationship with money look like to you?

August 13th

When have you felt at your richest?

August 14th

Do you prefer physical money (cash) or digital money (cards/cryptocurrencies)?

August 15th

What is the largest sum of money you've ever received?

August 16th

What, in your opinion, is a "good" amount of money to earn?

August 17th

What was your parents' attitude towards money? How has this influenced you today?

August 18th

What is the most money you've ever spent on something?

August 19th

What would you do with your time if money were no object?

August 20th

Imagine you inherited $5000 from a distant relative with the condition you had to spend it on something other than yourself. What would you do with the money?

August 21st

What would you do if you ran out of money tomorrow?

August 22nd

When have you felt at your poorest?

August 23rd

What is the best or most helpful piece of advice you've heard about money? And the worst?

August 24th

"Time is more valuable than money." - Jim Rohn. What do you think about this statement?

August 25th

What would you do differently today if you took 10% more responsibility for your relationship with money?

August 26th

If you had a choice between receiving $200 now or $2000 in six months' time, which would you choose? Why?

August 27th

How do you talk about money with friends and family?

August 28th

What would you like your financial life to look like in 10 years' time?

August 29th

What do you think about the saying "Money is the root of all evil?"

August 30th

What feels unresolved in your financial life right now? What can you do to resolve this?

August 31st

What is one thing you could do today to improve your financial life?

REVIEWING AUGUST

Does money make your world go around? Or is it something you wish didn't exist? Whatever your feelings about money, you've unpacked and explored them this month. Money can be a tricky topic for many people. I hope now, at the end of this month, you have a clearer sense of your relationship to money and your beliefs around it and have begun to make peace with your money story, past and present. As you think about your money-related journaling from this month, consider the following questions:

- What did I learn about myself this month?
- Which of the prompts this month were most challenging?
- Which of my answers most surprised me?
- Based on what I've written, one action I want to take over the next month is…

PART 9

SEPTEMBER: TRAVEL AND ADVENTURE

September 1st

Create a bucket list of things you'd like to do, see, and experience during your lifetime.

September 2nd

Make a list of places you want to visit.

September 3rd

What does adventure mean to you?

September 4th

How can you find adventure at home today?

September 5th

What are your favorite travel memories?

September 6th

What places in the world have meaning or significance
to you?

September 7th

What kind of adventure would you never want to undertake?

September 8th

Which do you believe is more important: the journey or the
destination?

September 9th

Where have you felt most like a stranger or outsider? Why?

September 10th

What do you love about traveling?

September 11th

What do you despise about traveling?

September 12th

Where would you never visit, and why?

September 13th

What is the most adventurous thing you've done in your life so far?

September 14th

What brings you comfort when you're away from home?

September 15th

What is one way you can add more adventure to your daily life this week?

September 16th

Who is (or has been) your favorite person to travel with?

September 17th

Where have you been that feels like home away from home?

September 18th

What have you learned about yourself from your adventures so far?

September 19th

Describe the worst trip you've ever taken.

September 20th

Write about one interesting or unexpected experience you've had because of travel or adventuring—at home or abroad.

September 21st

Describe the best trip you've ever taken.

September 22nd

Where are your ancestral roots? Have far are you from them now?

September 23rd

What is your favorite mode of transport and why?

September 24th

Imagine someone called you tomorrow saying you'd won a round-the-world ticket (and it was legit!). Where would you go and why?

September 25th

What was the last trip you took? What was it like?

September 26th

What languages do you speak (or would you like to speak)?

September 27th

Describe one or more interesting people you've met through traveling.

September 28th

What have you gained through travel? And what have you
lost along the way?

September 29th

How do you plan an adventure: have everything ready down
to the smallest detail? Show up and see what happens?
Something in between?

September 30th

What will your next adventure be?

LOOKING BACK AT SEPTEMBER

It's a big, wide, world out there, and chances are we'll only see a fraction of it. As we've explored this month, however, adventure starts at home. Over the last 30 days, you've uncovered more about your relationship to adventure, your feelings, and experiences around travel, and discovered what kind of role you want these things to play in your future. It's time to review! Here are a few questions to consider as you think back on your responses from this month:

- What did I learn about myself this month?
- Which of the prompts this month were most challenging?
- Which of my answers most surprised me?
- Based on what I've written, one action I want to take over the next month is…

PART 10
OCTOBER: HEALTH

October 1st

How is your physical health right now?

October 2nd

How is your mental health today?

October 3rd

How do you feel about exercise?

October 4th

What is one thing you could start doing today to improve your physical health?

October 5th

What is one thing you could stop doing today to improve your physical health?

October 6th

What is one thing you could start doing today to improve your mental health?

October 7th

What is one thing you could stop doing today to improve your
mental health?

October 8th

List 10 of your favorite self-care activities. When was the last time you did each of them?

October 9th

If you were to take 10% better care of yourself today, what would you do differently?

October 10th

If your body could talk to you today, what would it say?

October 11th

What makes you feel energized?

October 12th

When do you feel most drained?

October 13th

How satisfying is your self-care practice these days?

October 14th

Describe a time when you felt at your physical peak.

October 15th

How do you feel about your eating habits these days?

October 16th

Make a list of 10 physical activities or hobbies you'd like to try one day.

October 17th

What is your number one health-related goal or wish right now?

October 18th

How do you think your emotions and beliefs affect your physical health?

October 19th

If this area of your life (health) were 100% ideal, what would that look like?

October 20th

What is the most useful health advice you've heard?

October 21st

What dietary philosophy (e.g. vegetarian, paleo, gluten-free, etc.) do you follow when it comes to your eating choices, and why?

October 22nd

How do you take care of your emotional health when you're angry, upset or hurt?

October 23rd

What would your ideal "mental health day" look like?

October 24th

As you think back on the last week, what are the predominant feelings you remember experiencing?

October 25th

What would you like your predominant feelings to be over the next week? What can you do to create those feelings?

October 26th

Where do you carry the most tension in your body? And in your life? What can you do to let some of this tension go?

October 27th

How's your sleep quality these days?

October 28th

What is the number one thing you can do today to feel more relaxed?

October 29th

Make a list of health stepping stones, the key health-related events in your life up to today.

October 30th

What do you think about the alternative health movement?

October 31st

Between your physical and mental health, which do you feel
needs the most attention today?

REFLECTING ON OCTOBER

This month's prompts have been all about your physical and mental health. Wherever you fall on the health spectrum—super duper fit and healthy or struggling with one or more ailments—it's valuable to reflect on your approach to your health, how you treat your physical self, and how you take care of your mind. Let's review your journaling from this month. As you look back over your answers, ask yourself:

- What did I learn about myself this month?
- Which of the prompts this month were most challenging?
- Which of my answers most surprised me?
- Based on what I've written, one action I want to take over the next month is…

PART 11

NOVEMBER: SPIRITUALITY

November 1st

What big things are you most grateful for right now?

November 2nd

What does spirituality mean to you?

November 3rd

Where does your spiritual streak show up in your daily life?

November 4th

What do you believe makes the world a better place?

November 5th

What practices feed your spiritual side?

November 6th

What has your spiritual journey been to this point?

November 7th

What are three small things you're grateful for today?

November 8th

Do you believe you find your purpose or believe your purpose finds you?

November 9th

Do you believe you have a soul? Why or why not?

November 10th

How do you feel about eating meat?

November 11th

Do you believe in any kind of god or creator?

November 12th

What gives your life meaning today? What leaves you feeling purposeful?

November 13th

Do you agree with the statement "Everything happens for a reason?" Why, or why not?

November 14th

What people, figures, or ideas have had the biggest impact on your spiritual life?

November 15th

What is the number one problem you would like to solve in the world?

November 16th

Describe a recent good deed or random act of kindness you undertook.

November 17th

What does courage look like to you?

November 18th

Do you think happiness is something you find or create?

November 19th

What do you think happens when we die?

November 20th

How do you define wisdom? Where do you look for wisdom in your own life?

November 21st

What do you think about the idea of a higher self?

November 22nd

What causes do you believe in?

November 23rd

When have you felt most connected to your spiritual side?

November 24th

Do you think tending to your spiritual side is important? Why
(or why not)?

November 25th

What are some of the mantras or guiding principles you use in your spiritual life?

November 26th

Do you believe more in serendipity or coincidence? Why?

November 27th

What is one thing you could start doing today to strengthen your sense of spirituality and your spiritual life?

November 28th

What do you think about the idea that we are all connected in some kind of metaphysical way?

November 29th

What are some of your biggest unanswered questions in life?

November 30th

How do you deal with life's uncertainties and unknowns?

A REVIEW OF NOVEMBER

Your spiritual self informs your beliefs about the world, your purpose, your place in the bigger puzzle of life, and more. Spirituality can involve religion, but it doesn't have to. It's how you make sense of the world, where you find joy, and what you feel gives your life meaning. I hope you've found it helpful to consider this aspect of your life over the last 30 days. This is a great time to review your responses to this month's prompts. As you do so, consider:

- What did I learn about myself this month?
- Which of this month's prompts were most challenging?
- Which of my answers most surprised me?
- Based on what I've written, one action I want to take over the next month is...

PART 12

DECEMBER: THE FUTURE

December 1st

What do you think of when you think about "the future?"

December 2nd

What would you like to learn about in the next year?

December 3rd

What advice do you think the 80-year-old version of yourself
would have for the you of today?

December 4th

Where would you like to be in 20 years?

December 5th

Write a letter to yourself in 10 years time. Include all your hopes, dreams, plans, and aspirations for the future.

December 6th

If you lived each day as you did today, what do you think your future would look like?

December 7th

If you had to set one intention for the week ahead, what would it be?

December 8th

How would you like to feel over the next month? What can you do to make that happen?

December 9th

How would you like to be thought of and remembered by your family and friends in years to come?

December 10th

In which areas of your life does your future feel foggy?

December 11th

What are your biggest ideas right now? Which ideas just won't leave you alone? Give them a voice here, today.

December 12th

What is one thing you'd like to have more of in the future, and one thing you'd like to have less of?

December 13th

Imagine you are reading this one year from now...

- *Where are you?*
- *What are some of the highlights from the past 12 months?*
- *What is different, and what is the same?*
- *What do you feel proudest about from the year just gone?*

December 14th

How do you think the world will be different in 10 years time?

December 15th

What are some of the things you are doing in your life today that will impact your future?

December 16th

Describe a recent challenging situation and how you handled it. What did you learn from this that could be useful for future challenges?

December 17th

Imagine you could time travel and found yourself 50 years in the future. What would you hope to find?

December 18th

What are some of your biggest questions about the future (these can be about your life or the world in general)?

December 19th

How do you feel about death?

December 20th

What is your biggest hope for the future?

December 21st

What is your biggest fear for the future?

December 22nd

What is one thing you want to do, experience, or achieve before you die?

December 23rd

If you could ask yourself 10 years in the future one question, what would it be?

December 24th

What would you like to remember about today?

December 25th

At the end of your life, how will you know if your time here has been a success?

December 26th

What is something you've done or experienced in the past you don't want to repeat in the future?

December 27th

Which of your personal strengths would you like to build on in the future?

December 28th

What could you do today that your future self would most thank you for?

December 29th

Think of an upcoming event, situation or time when you know you'll need extra support, cheerleading or a pep talk. Write a letter to your future self, sharing everything you'd like to share.

You can also adapt this prompt and write a letter to yourself to open on the eve of the next new year, your next birthday, a significant anniversary, or any other important date or milestone.

December 30th

How would you like to deepen your journaling over the next year?

December 31st

What would you like your theme for this next year to be?

LOOKING BACK AT DECEMBER

The end of the year is traditionally a time of reflection and planning, which is why this month's prompts were all about the future. You've explored your hopes and dreams, discovered how to seek inspiration from your older, wiser self, and deepened your awareness about what you want your next year to look like. As you reflect on what you've written this month, take a few moments to ask yourself:

- What did I learn about myself this month?
- Which of the prompts this month were most challenging?
- Which of my answers most surprised me?
- Based on what I've written, one action I want to take over the next month is…

PART 13

LOOKING BACK ON YOUR YEAR OF YOU

You made it a year! Congratulations. Whether you started the prompts in January, May, or November, completing 365 days of journaling (or close enough!) is a celebration-worthy feat.

What to do now? You can always return to day one and journal another year of you, either in a separate notebook or in a new copy of this book. As you go, you might find it interesting to look back on your answers from the year before to see what's changed (and how it's changed) and what's stayed the same over the past 365 days.

Before you do so, this a great opportunity to think about how cultivating this journaling habit has impacted your life over the last year. What has changed in your life because of your year of you? What are you doing differently? More of? Less of? How do you feel *you* have changed?

If you'd like to expand your journaling repertoire, you can find dozens of journaling prompts, tips, and techniques in my book *The Ultimate Guide to Journaling*. You can also find a bounty of inspiration for journaling on social media platforms like Pinterest and Facebook.

In the next two chapters, I'm sharing my favorite templates for doing a weekly, monthly, and annual review—an addition to my journaling practice I've found helpful for living as consciously and fully as possible. You will also find a list of resources and recommended reading that will allow you to explore the different areas of your life further.

If you enjoyed this book, please consider sharing a review on Amazon, Goodreads, or the website from which you purchased your copy. Your reviews are invaluable for indie authors like me and will help other potential readers decide if *The Year of You* is right for them. If you have any comments on suggestions about this book, I would love to hear more about your experience. Feel free to get in touch with me and share your thoughts: hannah@becomingwhoyouare.net.

Thank you—and congratulations again—for taking this journey with me over the past year. I hope it's been enjoyable and enriching and that you will have many fulfilling years of writing to come.

Hannah

PART 14
EXTRAS

BONUS PROMPTS: THE WEEKLY, MONTHLY, AND ANNUAL REVIEW

In this chapter, I want to share a way of supplementing your regular journaling using a weekly, monthly, and/or annual review. The questions and frameworks I'm about to share will fit alongside your daily journaling practice (if you decide to do another *Year of You!*), or you might choose to use them as a way of continuing your journaling habit. Weekly, monthly, and annual reviews have helped me stay in touch with all aspects of my life and figure out how well (or not) they're melding. I love having side projects and, at any given time, have several on the go, plus more ideas in my head. Making time for a regular review helps me stay focused on what I want, keep some semblance of balance in my life, and be conscious about decisions I make and how I spend my time. You don't have to do all three if you don't want to. I used to, and I'm sharing the templates I used for all three here. Since I became a mother and my priorities changed, however, I find doing monthly and annual reviews sufficient.

The weekly and monthly reviews are simple (since I do them regularly, I find the simpler the better), while my annual review is more involved. I do my weekly and monthly reviews on the same day of each week or month, and I make my annual review a special occasion, taking an afternoon or longer to do it.

I find it helpful to do all three using the following prompts as a framework. That's what works for me; what works for you might be different. You might adapt some of the prompts, exclude some, and add others. I've worked with clients who found it helpful to skip weekly reviews and just do them monthly as well as clients who also added a shorter daily review to their routine too. As with all things journaling-related, the "right" way to do this will be personal to you, so go ahead and make it your own!

Weekly review

My weekly review is five simple questions I use to check in with myself. I arrived at these five particular questions as I wanted to encapsulate all areas of my life without over-complicating the review process.

1. Three good things that happened this week:
2. What worked over the last 7 days?
3. What didn't (and what can I learn from this)?
4. What do I want to be mindful of next week?
5. In one week's time, I would like to have…
   (done/felt/seen/watched/met/etc…)

Monthly review

My monthly review is longer as a lot can happen in a month. Again, I try to encapsulate the different areas of my life—personal and professional—to keep the review process as straightforward as possible.

1. Top goals/primary outcomes for the year:
2. What did I accomplish this month? (professional and personal)
3. Notable events and happenings
4. What I read this month (and books in progress):
5. What I listened to this month (music, audiobooks, podcasts, etc.):
6. What I watched this month (TV, movies, videos):
7. What do I feel proud of from the last month?
8. What was challenging this month?
9. What lessons did I learn?
10. What do I want to accomplish next month? (and how does this fit with my goals for the year?)

Annual review

As you're about to see, my annual review goes deep and involves looking at each area of my life individually, reflecting on my progress so far and deciding how I'd like to focus on that area going forward. I find it's helpful to make an occasion out of doing this review at the end of the calendar year, however you could also do this around your birthday or another annual milestone that has personal significance for you.

1. Start your personal end-of-year review by reflecting on the different areas of life

These are:

- Job/career
- Health and fitness
- Finances
- Family
- Romance/dating
- Friendships

- Fun and leisure
- Home/physical environment
- Personal growth and development

For each area, answer the following questions:

1. What worked this year?
2. What is still a work in progress in this area?
3. What are the wins from this area of life over the past year?
4. And the mishaps?
5. Where are the gaps between what I'm saying I want in this area of life and how I'm living it?
6. What lessons have I learned from this area of life over the past year?
7. How do I feel about each area when I think about the past year?
8. How do I want to feel about each area this time next year?
9. Who do I want to be in this area of my life over the next year? What qualities do I want to embody?

2. Choose 3 of the above areas to focus on over the next six months

There are two ways to make this choice. If you have specific areas of life that need some TLC, it might be a good idea to focus on these first. If things are going well across the board, consider choosing the areas with the most potential or that would excite you to focus on.

For each of the three areas you've chosen, consider the following questions:

- Where would I ideally like to be with each of these areas in a year's time?

- What do I need to do to get there? What tangible steps do I need to take to make those things happen?
- How will I know when I get there? How can I measure my progress?
- What do I need to learn? Are there any knowledge gaps I need to address to take these steps?
- Who could be useful for support/guidance? Who do I know who is already rocking these areas of life? And how might they be able to support me? (Note: these don't have to be people you know personally, they can be people whose books you read, people who model who you'd like to become and how you'd like to show up in the world, and public figures you admire.)
- What do I think are likely to be my three biggest obstacles as I take these steps?
- What can I do in other areas of my life to support these steps? (For example, let's say improving your health and fitness is a goal and going to the gym three times a week is one of the tangible steps. A complementary habit might be making sure you go to bed by a certain time so you can get up early to work out.)
- Who do I need to become to live this vision? What qualities will that version of myself embody?

3. Create your roadmap

This is an important part of the personal end-of-year review that we often miss out on. Decide now when and how often you will take those tangible steps and schedule them into your calendar. Here are two suggestions to help:

Focus on making this sustainable.

Using the gym example above, going from zero visits per week straight up to five visits per week is unlikely to last. Start with one or two visits and build up from there. Remember: there is no rush and diving into extremes is often a not-so-subtle form of self-sabotage. Make it as easy as possible for yourself to succeed.

Focus on one change at a time.

This is also about giving yourself the best chance of success. Once the first change has become your new "normal," then you can move on to something else. Trying to change all three areas of your life at once and in one go could overwhelm and hinder your progress more than it will help.

4. Let go of your vision

Having created a vision in part 2, I now invite you to let go of it. Why? Because the only thing you can control is the process and your input, not the outcome. Your vision is also likely to change and evolve as you make progress throughout the year. As you make progress, you might discover that certain goals are no longer as relevant or important as they once felt. As important as qualities like consistency and tenacity are, we need to let go of plans and goals that are no longer right for us. Having a general sense of where you're heading is helpful, but the only thing you need to focus on is the next tangible step.

As I mentioned at the beginning of this chapter, I've found reviewing each week, month, and year invaluable. I've also tweaked and adjusted my reviews as I go to fit my life and my preferences.

This chapter marks the end of the prompts in this book. In the next section, you'll find resources and recommended reading to go with each month's prompts.

RECOMMENDED READING AND ADDITIONAL RESOURCES

To finish up, I want to share some tools, resources, and reading you might find useful as a complement to the personal exploration you do during your Year of You. These tools and books fit one or more of the topics you're covering month-by-month and will help you deepen your self-awareness further.

Tools and Resources

The Becoming Who You Are Library. Get free workbooks, audios, and video classes to continue your personal growth: http://library.becomingwhoyouare.net/

VIA strengths test: http://www.viacharacter.org/www/Character-Strengths-Survey

750words.com. If you want motivation and accountability for regular journaling, 750words.com is a great tool. As well as having a dedicated space to write each day, you can keep track of your journaling streak, unlock fun badges based on your journaling habits, and see useful stats about your writing: http://750words.com

Day One Journaling App/Software: http://dayoneapp.com/

Books

The following list contains books I recommend that are relevant to the different areas of life covered in *The Year of You*. You can find direct links to all these books by visiting http://www.becomingwhoyouare.net/year-of-you

The Gifts of Imperfection: Let Go of Who You Think You're Supposed to Be and Embrace Who You Are by Brené Brown

Daring Greatly: How the Courage to Be Vulnerable Transforms the Way We Live, Love, Parent, and Lead by Brené Brown

On Becoming a Person: A Therapist's View of Psychotherapy by Carl Rogers

Games People Play: The Basic Handbook of Transactional Analysis by Eric Berne

The 5 Love Languages: The Secret to Love that Lasts by Gary D. Chapman

Gifts Differing: Understanding Personality Type - Isabel Briggs Myers and Peter B. Myers

Getting the Love You Want: A Guide for Couples by Harville Hendrix

Nonviolent Communication: A Language For Life by Marshall Rosenberg

Journal to the Self: 22 Paths to Personal Growth by Kathleen Adams

Start Where You Are: A Guide to Compassionate Living by Pema Chodron

The Places That Scare You: A Guide to Fearlessness in Difficult Times by Pema Chodron

Overcoming Underearning: A 5-Step Plan to a Richer Life by Barbara Stanny

A Creative Guide to Exploring Your Life: Self-Reflection Using Photography, Art, and Writing by Graham Gordon Ramsey and Holly Barlow Sweet

Boundaries: Where You End and I Begin - How to Recognize and Set Healthy Boundaries by Anne Katherine

The Six Pillars of Self-Esteem: The Definitive Work on Self-Esteem by the Leading Pioneer in the Field by Nathaniel Branden

Self-Compassion: The Proven Power of Being Kind to Yourself by Kristin Neff

The Artist's Way by Julia Cameron

Writing Alone Together: Journalling in a Circle of Women for Creativity, Compassion and Connection by Ahaha Shira, Wendy Judith Cutler, and Lynda Monk

The Happiness Advantage: The Seven Principles That Fuel Success and Performance at Work by Shawn Achor

The Power of TED* (*The Empowerment Dynamic) by David Emerald

The Happiness Hypothesis: Finding Modern Truth in Ancient Wisdom by Jonathan Haidt

Succeed: How we can Reach our Goals by Heidi Grant Halvorson

ALSO BY HANNAH BRAIME

The Ultimate Guide to Journaling

In *The Ultimate Guide to Journaling*, **you'll find the tips, inspiration, and prompts you need to start and maintain a journaling practice for DIY self-discovery.** This clear and concise handbook shares everything you need to know to deepen your relationship with yourself using this powerful personal development tool. Covering foundational topics like how to journal, which tools to use, and how to make it a regular habit, as well as over 30 different journaling techniques and many more prompts, *The Ultimate Guide to Journaling* will help you keep your practice flowing for years to come.

From Coping to Thriving: How to Turn Self-Care Into a Way of Life

From Coping to Thriving **is a comprehensive guide to making self-care part of your everyday life.** With a balance between practical suggestions, coaching-style questions and psychological groundwork, this book is designed to give you the self-knowledge and awareness you need to start making self-care an integral part of your life. Not only does *The Ultimate Guide to Journaling* contain hundreds of useful self-care tips and ideas, it will also take you deeper into related topics like habit-formation, coping strategies, dealing with resistance to self-care and more.

The Power of Self-Kindness: How to Transform Your Relationship with Your Inner Critic

In *The Power of Self-Kindness: How to Transform Your Relationship With Your Inner Critic*, **you'll discover a radical approach to healing your relationship with your inner critic and yourself, one based on understanding, self-acceptance and self-compassion.**

Using a combination of theory, insight and reflective practices, you'll learn where your critic comes from and how to look beyond its destructive words to uncover the real message underneath. You'll develop techniques that will help you question your critic's stories and become more mindful of how these stories impact your life. You'll also learn how to turn up the volume on the inner critic's positive counterpart - the inner mentor - a wise inner guiding light invested in your growth and wellbeing.

Whether you've been struggling with your inner critic for a long time or are at the beginning of your self-kindness journey, this book offers a range of approaches and suggestions you can use to mend the most important relationship in your life: the one with yourself.

ABOUT THE AUTHOR

Hannah Braime is a creative life coach and author, who writes about journaling, self-care, and creativity. She is the author of two other books, *The Ultimate Guide to Journaling* and *From Coping to Thriving: How to Turn Self-Care Into a Way of Life*. She also shares practical psychology-based articles and resources on creating a full and meaningful life with greater courage, compassion, and authenticity at www.becomingwhoyouare.net.

Stay in touch to hear more about future books:
www.becomingwhoyouare.net
hannah@becomingwhoyouare.net

ACKNOWLEDGMENTS

I would like to express my gratitude to everyone who contributed to this book, directly and indirectly.

Special thanks to Jake and Stephanie for their feedback, suggestions, and support; to Jake again for his encouragement, willingness to talk at length about the moving parts of this book, and patience as I spent many evenings tapping away on my computer; thanks to Freya for bringing so much joy into the world and reminding me what matters most in life; the friends and readers who gave their feedback and suggestions regarding the title and cover, and everyone else who supported and encouraged the publication of this book.

Thank you also to the writers and teachers I don't know personally, but whose books, blogs, podcasts, and wisdom have influenced and inspired me to keep journaling, keep writing, and to keep doing what I can to leave my tiny corner of the world better off than I found it.

Made in the USA
Middletown, DE
07 May 2020